The Only Affiliate Marketing Book Worth Reading

Actionable Tips To Help You Reach A $10,000 Monthly Revenue Without Having A Website (Learn How To Avoid Common Mistakes)

Justin A. Parker

Bluesource And Friends

This book is brought to you by Bluesource And Friends, a happy book publishing company.

Our motto is **"Happiness Within Pages"**

We promise to deliver amazing value to readers with our books.

We also appreciate honest book reviews from our readers.

Connect with us on our Facebook page www.facebook.com/bluesourceandfriends and stay tuned to our latest book promotions and free giveaways.

Don't forget to claim your FREE books!

Brain Teasers:

https://tinyurl.com/karenbrainteasers

Harry Potter Trivia:

https://tinyurl.com/wizardworldtrivia

Sherlock Puzzle Book (Volume 2)

https://tinyurl.com/Sherlockpuzzlebook2

Also check out our best seller books

"67 Lateral Thinking Puzzles"

https://tinyurl.com/thinkingandriddles

"Rookstorm Online Saga"

https://tinyurl.com/rookstorm

Introduction

Hello and welcome to *The Only Affiliate Marketing Book Worth Reading!*

I would like to thank you for getting this book and I hope that it will be useful in helping you build up your own online business! And I also want to congratulate you! We are all better off when people get bold and take control of their own future by starting a business, so I congratulate you on taking the first step!

Affiliate marketing is a very exciting way to have your own online business. It's by far the easiest way to get started with a legitimate online business that actually makes good money. Some people actually make *millions* of dollars selling affiliate products online. Of course, that's not our goal in this book right now since you're just getting started. But, making a $10,000-a-month income is not far-fetched at all!

The problem for most people is they have no idea where to start. But I am going to show you how to do it in this book.

I understand the business. I've been an affiliate marketer and have had my own products, using other people as affiliates to help me push it.

Several years back, I actually had my own product that I sold through an affiliate program called Clickbank, something we're going to talk about in this book. After you get an affiliate marketing business going, you may want to develop a product of your own. When you do that, you can really skyrocket your income.

But we're getting ahead of ourselves. It's certainly not necessary to develop your own product if that is not your thing. You absolutely don't need to have your own product, and you can make $100, $200, and even $300 a day or more selling other people's products as an affiliate.

And you can earn this money as a passive income. Meaning that you set it up and it runs itself, giving you a way to earn money while you sleep, spend time with your family, or relax on a vacation. It sounds too good to be true, right? It isn't!

Now if you're just looking to earn a little bit of extra money, affiliate marketing is definitely a great way to do that. With small investments of time and money, you can generate income of up to $50, $500, $1000, or even $2500 a month without having to work full-time. Imagine being able to make your car payment or your house payment without having to take a second job.

Affiliate marketing allows you to do that.

The huge advantage of affiliate marketing is that you can find products that are *already selling*. That is what we're going to teach about in this book.

When you find a product that is already selling, all you have to do is send them web traffic. Then they do all the rest. And the beauty is that since you know that the product is already selling, you're definitely going to get sales.

The easiest affiliate products to deal with are online digital products. We're going to be showing you how to find them, determine which ones to sell, and then start making money pushing them yourself. There are also many other ways to make money as an affiliate, including becoming an affiliate for big sites like Amazon.com and some other options. No matter which path you choose, it's definitely possible to start earning an income online very quickly.

The problem that most people have is that they aren't sure where to start. But we are going to show you how to begin in this book, giving you the exact steps to follow.

Let's not waste any more time, turn the page over to get started!

Chapter 1: What is Affiliate Marketing?

Boy, it sure would be nice to have passive income.

Imagine banking in $100 a day in your sleep, or while you are at the movies, or having dinner with friends.

Sounds crazy, right?

The thing is, it's not crazy at all. That kind of income is well within your reach if you carefully follow the steps I am going to outline in this book. Making passive income online is not only possible, but it's also easier than it ever has been before. That might sound a bit crazy since the internet has grown massive and competition is fierce. But it's true – you just have to know the tricks and secrets that I'm going to show you in this book.

What is Exactly is Affiliate Marketing?

So what is affiliate marketing?

First off, I want to make it clear that this is not some kind of multi-level marketing or pyramid scam. If anyone tries to pay you for recruiting your family and friends to a "business", run!

Affiliate marketing is a genuine and legal way to make money. And it takes place entirely online, so you won't even have to tell your friends that you're even doing it, much less try and push it on them. Of course, when you start banking checks, you'll probably want to tell them about it so they can start making money themselves.

The way it works is online businesses – often publishers but also big websites like Amazon will pay you a commission for sending them traffic.

So what you do is you drive traffic to the site, and then if the customer buys, you get a commission. In other words, you're a legitimate salesperson for the company, but it all takes place online. And you don't have to go out and sell stuff at all. Everything takes place online and it is all automated.

That isn't to say you can't take an active role in selling. Many people use techniques to sell products to get free traffic that we are going to talk about in this book.

But paid traffic is the best way to go. Fortunately, it is cheaper than EVER. If you're thinking you're going to blow thousands of dollars, you don't know how it works. Yeah, Google pay-per-click ads can be expensive, but there are so many ways to promote online these days that you can get thousands of eyeballs to your product without even bothering much with it.

Once you get started, you can take this as far as you want it to go. The beginning is the hardest part like in any endeavor, but let me tell you, once you figure out the secret sauce after that, it is pretty automatic.

Can You Become a Millionaire Online?

Some people are content to remain affiliate marketers. Believe it or not, you can make huge seven-figure incomes simply by doing affiliate marketing. There are many ways you can do it – you can push one high-ticket item, or promote multiple items simultaneously, building your business up slowly, or you can partner up with big online sellers and get huge commissions.

It has to be said - disclaimer coming - that a seven-figure income is definitely not typical. But I mentioned it to note that it is definitely possible. Whether or not you actually make that much depends on many factors, but the first factor is: How motivated you are, how persistent you are, how willing you are to learn and having a bit of savvy knowing what to sell and when to call it quits on specific products.

Some people use affiliate marketing to learn the ropes of running an online business, and then they create their own product. There are many ways that you can do this, for example, you can create a downloadable book on a niche topic, or make a video training course. Or if you are into physical products, you can open a Shopify store and dropship other peoples' products. Some even get bold and launch their own products they have manufactured overseas. Surprisingly, it's easier to do that than you think!

We won't be talking about that in this book, though. Our focus is on affiliate marketing. But once you get your own affiliate business up and running, you might want to go all-in and create your own product line and company.

Now while using Amazon and other big sites are ways you can earn some commission, my preference is for online digital products. The reason is that you can find many that pay high commissions. Some even pay $100 per sale, $500 per sale, and over $1,000 per sale. Of course, there is a trade-off; it is easier to convince someone to drop $40 than it is to convince them to drop $1,000. However, as you'll see, we can find products that cost money that sell, and then we can just send them traffic.

Sites to Look At

Now before we dive in, you need to be aware of some of the top sites that you can use to become an affiliate marketer. Ultimately, which site you decide to use will be up to you, but my preference is Clickbank, and we are going to be spending a lot of time discussing it. Of course, you can use multiple streams through all the sites as you go along. However, when you are just getting started, its best to focus on one thing and make it work before spreading yourself out all over the place. And as we'll see, Clickbank lets you get into virtually ANY niche, so it is not even necessary to look elsewhere.

Nonetheless, you'll want to check these out:

- https://www.clickbank.com/: One of the first if not the first online affiliate site, it has paid out billions of dollars in commissions.
- https://www.wealthyaffiliate.com/: A site that has built-in tools to help you create your own website and also as an affiliate.
- https://www.jvzoo.com/: Another affiliate program similar to Clickbank; also has options for joint ventures and product launches.

- https://affiliate-program.amazon.com/: Amazon, of course – the king of online business.
- https://partnernetwork.ebay.com/: eBay is an oldie but a goody. It still has massive traffic and provides a good way to make some side cash.
- https://www.shopify.com/affiliates: Shopify is a platform that helps people build their own online stores. You can send traffic over as an affiliate.
- https://www.clickfunnels.com/: Clickfunnels is a tool you may want to use to design your own web page and it's a site where you can earn money as an affiliate. Some people are earning six-figure sums a year just by pushing Clickfunnels, but it is now getting crowded.

There are many more. If you are interested in any large online business, simply type in the name of the business and "affiliate" in a Google search and you will find information on their affiliate programs if they have one.

Why Start With Digital?

So there are a few reasons why we will want to get started by pushing digital products. These include:

- Ease of use. With no shipping involved, you can often get quick impulse buys. Plus, transactions are instant and there are no hassles with inventory and shipping, and if there is a return, there is nothing to physically ship back.
- High commission. Would you rather get a few bucks getting an Amazon sale, or earn $500 from getting someone to sign up for an online video course?
- Focus on a niche (see below and the next chapter).
- Less competition. If a new gadget comes out on Amazon, it might be hard to stand out from the crowd. An online digital product will be sold from a site with a lot less traffic, but it's a less crowded space as well.
- Take advantage of your passions. What excites and interests you? The best way to do affiliate marketing is to pick out something that you are interested in talking about. This will make it fun to promote the product, rather than be tedious work. That will make it amenable to free-traffic methods. Digital products exist for any hobby, interest, or problem you can think of. So you can probably find your product of interest.

First Steps

In the next chapter, we are going to start discussing what you should sell. This is called "finding a niche", which is a narrowly-focused market. Think about retail in the city where you live – a niche could be women's clothing, while another niche might be hardware. Online, you can have a niche for virtually any hobby or interest. The best niche is one that solves some kind of problem that people are having. People are online all the time searching for solutions to their problems, and one of the easiest ways to get started as an online marketer is to be there when they are searching, offering them the exact solution they are looking for!

Chapter 2: Finding a Niche (Identifying a Burning Demand)

In this chapter, we are going to show you how to find a niche to target. Over time, you can build up your business by targeting multiple niche products if you want to. You can also make a big income only pushing one high-converting product. How you approach that is up to you, but in the beginning, you definitely want to start out focused. The key, of course, is to find something that is going to work. I advise people to pick something they are passionate about because that is going to make launching an online business that much easier. When you are interested in some topic, you're going to find it easy to spend time on it, and you might even want to devote time to driving free traffic. The word "free" is a misnomer because nothing in life is free. You are going to pay the price somewhere, and with "free" traffic you're going to pay the price in time spent developing an online presence to drive the traffic. And so you need to be interested in whatever you are doing so as to pull that off well.

It's going to be important to find some kind of balance. You want to find something that you are interested in that also sells well. You are also going to want to find something that sells but isn't overcrowded. Fortunately, Clickbank provides a huge amount of information about the products you can sell as an affiliate so there isn't much mystery.

Since Clickbank does give you so much information, it's a great place where you can learn how to become an affiliate marketer, so we are going to start from there and show you what you need to look for.

Solve a Problem

The way to approach niche marketing is to look for something that not only are you interested in, but also something that solves a specific problem for the customer. People are looking online for solutions to their problems, and they are willing to pay money to find a good solution. Many people are already online looking to buy a product RIGHT NOW. Of course, the key is to find them; we will talk about that later, but the main point is to focus on whether you want a problem-solving product.

Let's take "acne" as a quick example to illustrate: A book that goes into the physiology of acne might be interesting, especially if you have a passion for science and dermatology. But that isn't exactly what people who would want to solve a problem are looking for urgently, is it? They would want a book, ointment or video tutorial, etc. – something that will teach them HOW TO GET RID OF ACNE.

So your passion has to have some level of practicality to it as well. The more important the problem is to solve, the easier it is to sell something that fits the solution.

The Big, Evergreen Products

Now we don't want to restrict ourselves too much, and there are always tradeoffs to be made. But there are a few big niches which are "evergreen" – meaning that people are always willing to spend money on them. They were willing to spend money on them in 1950, 1980, and 2019, and they will be spending money on them in 2025, 2040 and 2050. You can probably guess what they are – people want to make money, lose weight, and they want to find a date!

So keep in mind the major evergreen niches:

- Make money (especially online)
- Weight loss
- Dating

The good news is that there is always money to be made in these three big areas. The tradeoff - and there is always a tradeoff - is that a lot of other people are also going to be marketing these products. But there is a lot of demand as well. There is an endless other side to the coin when considering the "big niche".

The good news is that there are multiple niches within a niche or sub-niches. Let's take a look at weight loss. I am sure that you can think of many different weight loss ideas and products right off the top of your head. Here are a few:

- Keto diet
- Lose 14 pounds in one week
- Diet pills
- Atkins diet
- Weight Watchers
- Low-fat diets
- Diabetes diets
- Mediterranean diet
- DASH diet

So you can narrow your focus and still use an evergreen niche, but be far more effective. Losing weight fast is something huge numbers of people are constantly searching for online.

But just targeting huge numbers of people isn't necessarily the best option. You want a large enough market so that, say, you can make more than one sale per month, but you don't want to be in an overcrowded space.

Google Trends

A great tool that you can use to gauge the feasibility of a niche is Google Trends. Go here:

https://trends.google.com/trends/

This won't give you absolute numbers, but you can see how something is trending with time. And then you can make comparisons. For example, this is what I get if I type in the phrase "make money online":

What's the first thing that stands out? For me, it's the stability of interest in a product. What this is indirectly telling us is the number of people that are searching this phrase online. The graph above shows us what it's been like for the past 12 months. We can also see what has happened over the past five years:

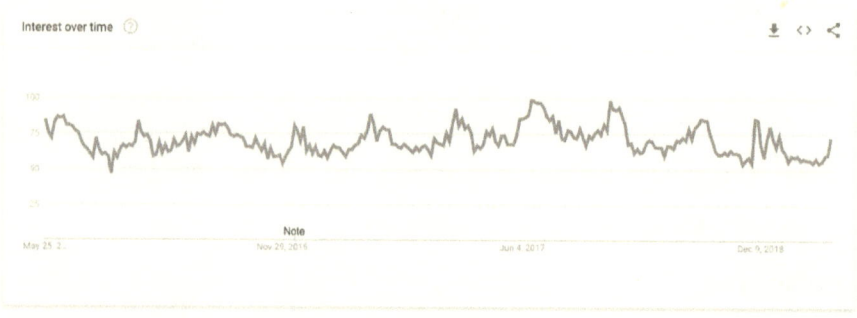

See what I mean by "evergreen"? There are a few mild ups and downs, but online interest in this topic is very constant.

Weight loss is also going to be pretty constant, but the current fad may or may not have legs for the long term. Let's look at the Keto diet for the past 12 months:

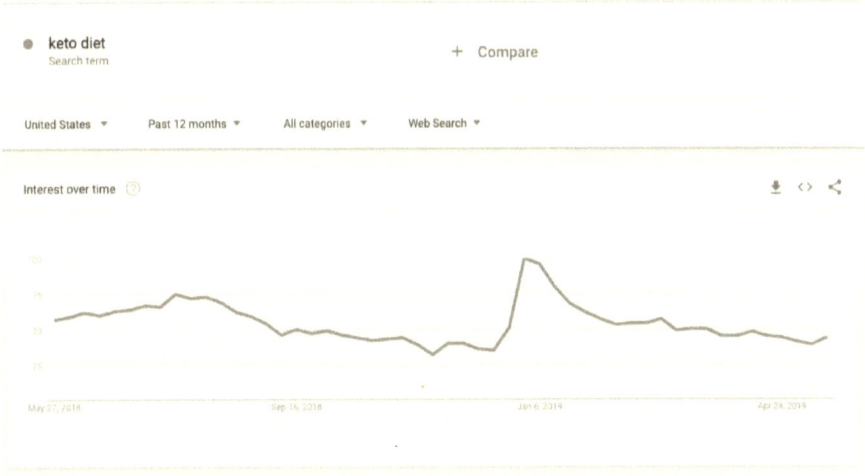

Unless you're living under a rock, you will know that the Keto diet is all the rage. It looks fairly steady over the past 12 months. It is hard to guess whether or not the Keto diet is really a "thing" and will be here for the long haul or whether it's just a fad. Truthfully, it doesn't matter. You can go all in and make money off the Keto diet now, but when things change and if they do, you can simply pivot to whatever new diet craze comes up. Over the past five years, we can see how the Keto diet has literally exploded in the last couple of years:

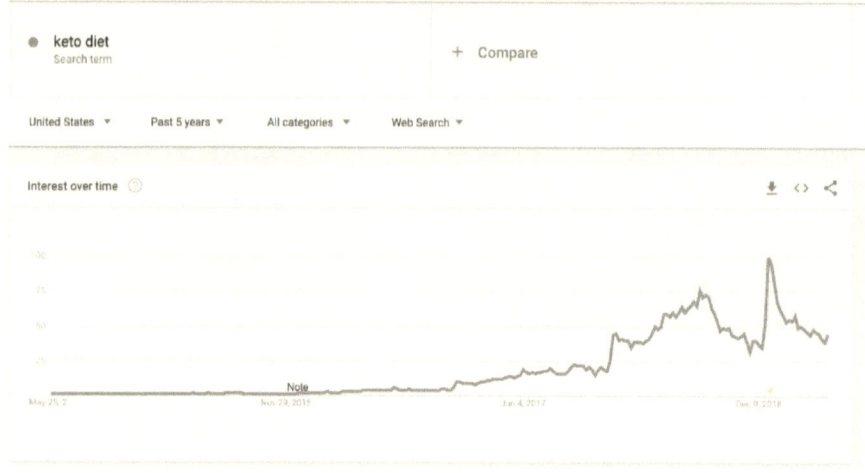

Searches for "Keto diet" literally went from nothing to one of the most popular searches on the web. Now, let us compare it to "Weight Watchers":

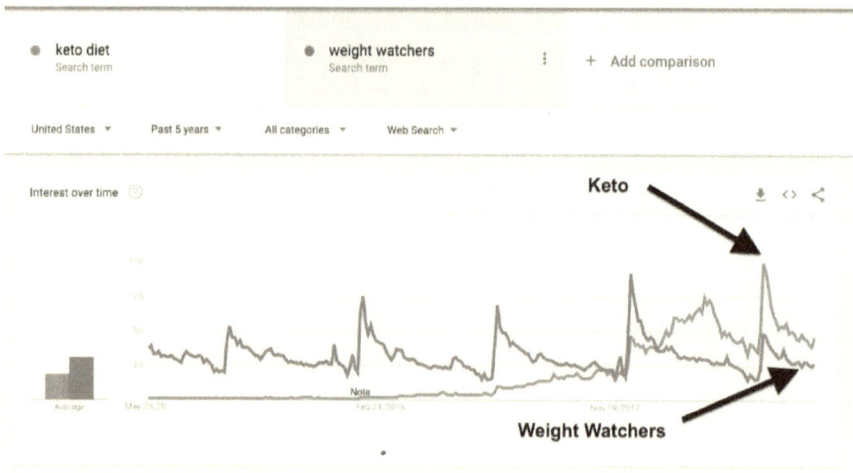

As you can see, "Weight Watchers" once dominated "Keto diet". But over the past 12 months, the Keto diet has *swamped* Weight Watchers. Google trends doesn't give you actual searches, but you can see a score or weight it assigns to each search term. In January of 2019, there were literally 2 searches for Keto diet for every search for weight watchers. That suggests that, right now at least, you are better off marketing a product that is aimed at people interested in the Keto diet (in fact, we will use that for our example in this chapter).

Something else to look for in Google Trends is how the search volume changes with time. You can see all those spikes in the weight loss searches, and you won't be surprised to know they happen every January. So at the beginning of the year, everyone resolves to lose weight, and they get online immediately when they are back from the holidays looking for solutions to the weight gain they've recently dealt with. You can use annual trends to figure out when to market your products in certain niches. Of course, for weight loss, while January can provide an opportunity for exploding sales, there is money to be made all year round.

The Clickbank Marketplace

The first stop when finding a niche is to visit the Clickbank marketplace. Before that, you will want to visit https://www.clickbank.com and create an account. Be sure to do everything you need for the account including entering your payment information so that you can actually get paid when you make your first sale!

To visit the marketplace, you will want to go here:

https://accounts.clickbank.com/marketplace.htm

This is where you will find all the products that are selling on Clickbank. On the left-hand side of the screen, you are going to see a list of general categories. You will see "Arts & Entertainment", "Business/Investing", "Home & Garden", and "Parents & Families", for example. Something to keep in mind is that every category has something that sells in it. So you are going to want to look for something you are interested in to find a product to promote. However, we are going to continue along with the "Keto diet" example to show you what you need to look out for.

At the top of the screen, you will find a search input box labeled "Find Products". You can type in any keyword you can think of to see if there are products available for that keyword. So I am going to type in "Keto diet" to see what comes up.

Now the screen looks like this – it has some results, sorted by keyword relevance:

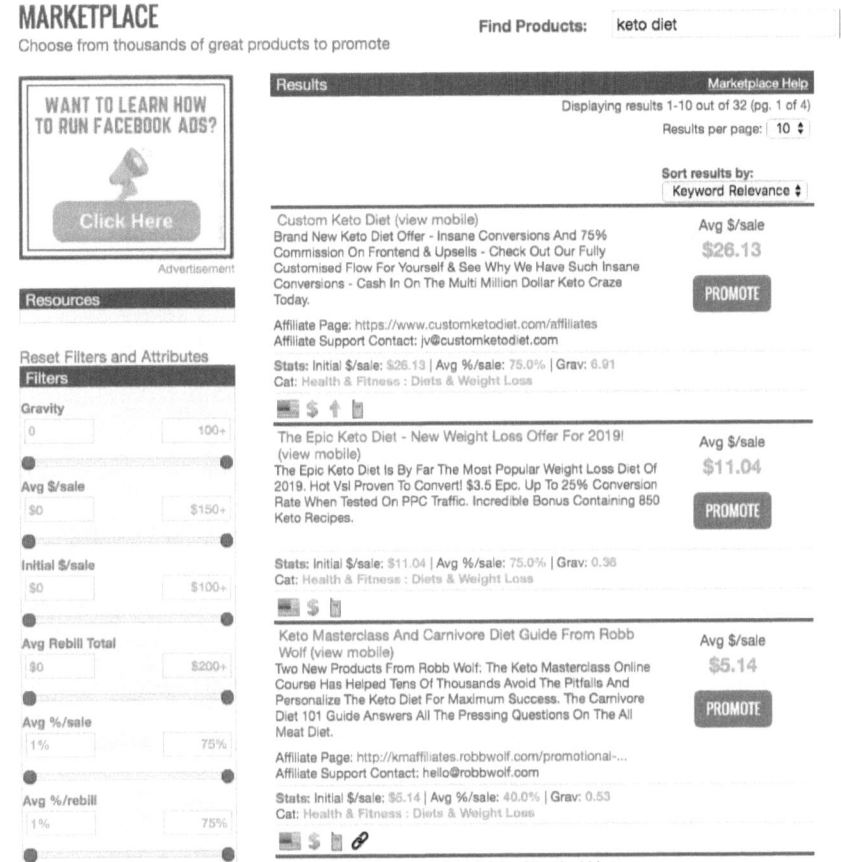

There are several options you can use for searching, including:

- Keyword relevance

- Popularity

- Gravity

- Average $/sale

And some other options too. The main ones you will want to focus on are "Average $/Sale" and the gravity. Now, "Average $/Sale" means what it says: This is the amount of money that you will make on average selling one copy of the product. The reason that it is quoted as an average is that oftentimes, retailers will add in upsells or subscriptions that you will also get credit for. So if some product sells for $47, but they offer an upgrade for $97 and 30% of their customers opt for the upgrade, that would give you the average earnings per sale.

Gravity

Gravity is one of the most important metrics to look for on Clickbank as an affiliate. This is a measure of how other affiliates are doing promoting this product. You might be interested in the product's popularity - and that can be an important measure too - but it is nice to know if other marketers are actually able to close sales. Popularity may be of interest, but that might be because the company selling the product is driving a lot of their own traffic.

So what is gravity? Gravity is a weighted measure of how many affiliates made sales over the past 12 weeks. Unfortunately, the actual formula is a secret, so we don't know in absolute terms if 5 people sold 7 copies of the product, or 3 people sold 100 copies of the product. Only Clickbank knows the actual details. But we do know that 1.0 means that at least one person made a sale. The number given is weighted, so a sale in the past few days gets a higher score than a sale from 5 weeks ago.

Luckily, experienced marketers have figured out the right gravity values to shoot for. These are guidelines and not hard and fast rules, so you don't *have* to pick a product using the suggested gravity values. Some new products might have a very low gravity or even 0.0 if they are just now hitting the market. Others might be undiscovered gems – very sellable products that haven't been promoted much by affiliates. You can use your own judgment by looking at the company's website and so on as you gain more experience, but in the beginning, its best to go with something that you know will sell. And the way to do that is to pick something that has a good gravity score.

Here are the guidelines to use:

- Pick a product that has a gravity of at least 20. That means it is getting solid, regular sales and affiliates are able to sell it.
- The gravity range should be between 20 to 80.
- The higher the gravity, the more competition you are going to face in the marketplace. A higher gravity score not only

means it's a hot seller, but it also means that there could be a large number of people selling it and promoting in on various platforms like Facebook and Google.

- When you're just starting out, avoid a gravity over 100, since that is a hot product that is going to be promoted by a lot of very experienced marketers – too much competition for a beginner.

- Make a match between gravity and price. A 20 gravity is nice, but if you only get a $6 commission per sale, that isn't going to help you even break even. You're going to probably want to look for products that sell from $30 and up.

Ok so now you have an idea what "gravity" means. When I sort "Keto diet" by gravity, here is what I find:

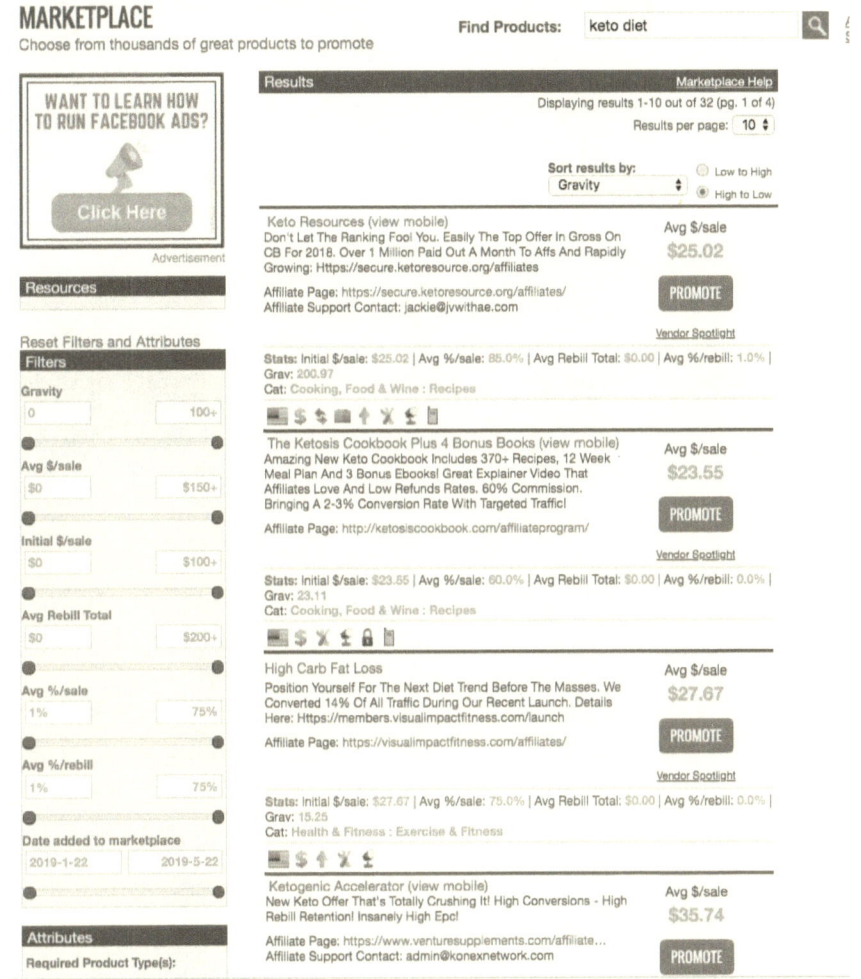

Notice that the top selling product, *"Keto Resources"*, has a super-high gravity of around 200. This is a hot selling product, and in the description, it notes that they are paying out $1 million a month to affiliates. However, the high gravity score might indicate that everyone and their brother are promoting this product. It could be worth a try, but you might have a better chance to make more money looking for something that has lower gravity, and so the market won't be as saturated. The high gravity score corresponds with what we found from Google Trends – "Keto diet" is a hot topic right now.

I also noticed something else – they have lowered the price of their product. It used to be $47 but now they are selling it for $37.

The next product, *"The Ketosis Cookbook"* only has a gravity of around 23. While the gravity of the top item is nearly 10 times higher, this is a perfect gravity for a beginning marketer. It means that the product is definitely something that sells, but there is less competition and so you won't be facing experienced "sharks" and the public won't feel as overwhelmingly saturated by it.

The next step once you've found something is to look at what the product offers for you as sales tools. You will also want to take a look at their website. First, let us take a look at how to get this information:

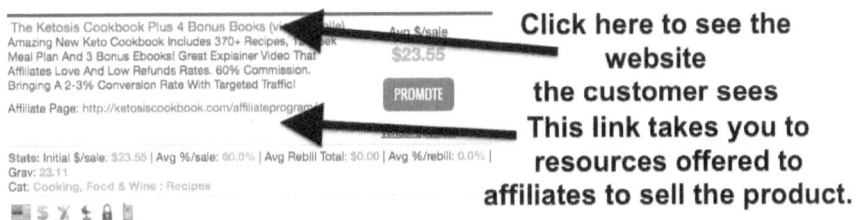

When browsing the Clickbank marketplace, you are going to find that some companies provide a lot of resources for affiliates while others provide hardly anything at all.

In fact, you will find that the top entry, *"Keto Resources"*, provides no assistance at all.

Some Companies Require Approval

When we click on the affiliate link for "The Ketosis Cookbook", we find that they are only accepting affiliates that they personally approve of. So we will bypass this product right now. They want you to document your traffic sources and so on, so they are looking to restrict their affiliates to experienced marketers that have some kind of online presence. The good news is that most Clickbank products don't require this kind of approval, and some that do require it is simply using the approval process as a filter and it is easy to get approved even if you don't have experience. Keep in mind that by the time you are finished reading this book, you should be able to get approval with a company like the one selling The Ketosis Cookbook because you will know what to tell them about traffic sources you are going to use, etc. When you contact them, you can lay that out in detail but state that you don't have it in place yet because you are new to the keto niche. You probably don't want to tell them that you've never done affiliate marketing at all beforehand. If you lay out a solid plan for traffic sources, they will probably be comfortable approving you because you sound like you know what you are doing.

To my surprise - and I am doing this in real time - the gravity drops off quite a bit after that. It is not really clear why but it may be because all the affiliates are going hard after the top item, which may have been the first product for Keto on Clickbank. For me, I might try one of the products with a lower gravity to see how it works out first, since the Keto diet is one of the hottest things going on these days. However, a beginner might continue searching for a product with a gravity of 20 or so that also has good affiliate resources to use.

Doing some more searching, I found a good dog training product. It has a gravity of 82, so it's a pretty good seller, but not as competitive as The Keto Resources product.

Brain Training For Dogs - Unique Dog Training Course! Easy Sell! (view mobile)
High Quality Dog Training Course Featuring 21 Games To Improve A Dog's Intelligence And Behavior, Plus Easy Instructions For Training Obedience Commands! Created By A Well Known Professional Dog Trainer! Affiliate Tools: Braintraining4dogs.com/affiliates

Affiliate Page: https://www.braintraining4dogs.com/affiliates/

Avg $/sale

$31.76

PROMOTE

Vendor Spotlight

Stats: Initial $/sale: $31.76 | Avg %/sale: 75.0% | Avg Rebill Total: $0.00 | Avg %/rebill: 1.0% | Grav: 82.86
Cat: Home & Garden : Animal Care & Pets

It also pays a commission per sale that is almost $32, which is pretty good. Clicking on the affiliate page, we see that they offer many useful tools that will help you promote the product. These include:

- Banners you can put on a blog or website of your own, and then link to the product.

- An email address so that you can contact them for help and advice.

- Explicit instructions on how to create your affiliate links to get credit for sales.

- Information about what the product does, which will help you sell the product. They also have a link to a professionally-written sales copy.

- Promotional videos that they allow you to use to market the product.

- Free giveaways (very important, as we will illustrate later).

- Email swipes.

- Keyword Ideas.

- A Facebook-lookalike audience.

In short, this product is a STELLAR example of what you are looking for. If you went with *The Keto Resources*, you would have to come up with all of this on your own, but these folks are providing you with everything you need to market products online.

Why Use Email Swipes

One of the best ways to promote an affiliate product is through email marketing. There are many ways that you can get people to give you their email addresses, but once you get them, you can automatically send them a series of emails to gradually sell the product. This has been a long time mainstay of online marketing and remains so to this day. Any product on Clickbank that provides you with email swipes are worth its weight in gold because that will save you a huge amount of time – they have already had professional sales copywriters develop emails that work and that can convert the product. We will talk more about this in a later chapter.

The Importance of a Facebook-Lookalike Audience

When you advertise on Facebook, they have an interesting and very powerful technology that is geared toward marketers. It is called a "lookalike audience". What you do is you upload a list of people that have already purchased a particular product, and then Facebook will analyze the list to find out what the characteristics of those people are. Then, it will create a new audience of people that has the same or similar characteristics. Those people are going to be hot to buy the same product! Any company on Clickbank that offers you a Facebook-lookalike audience is really helping you get a leg up in your marketing efforts – that will save you hundreds if not thousands of dollars in advertising expenses.

Free Giveaways

In our chapter on landing pages and "squeeze" pages, we will explore this in more detail, but a very popular marketing technique that works really well offers some sort of freebie in exchange for the person's email address. The fact that this company is offering giveaways that they have created is a huge help for you. These are quality products made by the same people that are free, and giving them away for free will actually convince many potential customers to buy the product. Typically, the company offering these items will have an automated way to insert your affiliate link into the document or whatever they are offering, so that you will be able to direct people to buy the product from inside the free giveaway.

In a Nutshell, What to Look For

So we've already decided that you should look for a product on Clickbank that has a gravity of at least 20. You should also look for one that has a gravity that isn't too high. I typically shoot for 20-80. When you go above 100, it is true that the product is selling but there may be a huge number of people selling it as well, making it a very competitive space to get into.

You also want to look for products that offer you many affiliate resources as well. All of the resources that we saw on the dog training website are very useful, but the main ones you want to look for are free giveaways and email swipes. Of course, you can also create your own. If you are a talented writer, you can write a short book on the topic at hand – maybe about 20 pages in length. Inside the book, you will include your affiliate links to the sales page for the main product. You should aim for quality – the purpose of the free book is to convince the prospect to buy the product so you don't want to just throw something together. In the chapter on emails, we will talk about how you might go about writing your own emails and how to get them sent out.

Another option is to visit Fiverr.com and hire someone to write a book for you. Carefully evaluate someone before hiring them. You want to make absolutely sure that they do quality work.

Getting Your Affiliate Link

Once you've settled on a product to promote, you are going to want to generate an affiliate link that you can use to send traffic to the sales page of the product. This is done by clicking on the red "PROMOTE" button.

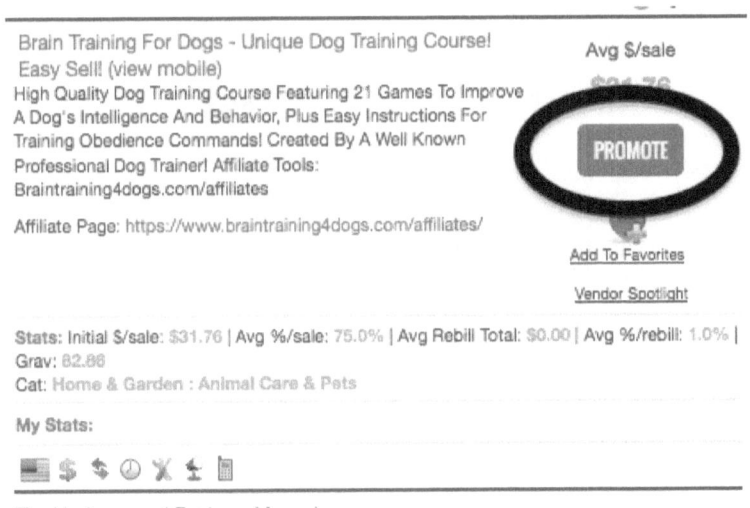

Make sure that you have already created your account before doing this, and that you have already logged into Clickbank. This will open a new screen that has your Clickbank user name in a form. That name will be used to identify your account with their technology when someone visits the web page and buys the product so that you get credit for the sale. Clickbank has been doing this for more than 20 years, so the technology is reliable. Click on "GET HOPLINKS" when the screen opens. If you want to have a tracking code, put a number or phrase in the optional tracking ID box. You might do this, for example, if you are sending traffic via Facebook and YouTube, and you want to know which one produces the most sales. When you generate your hoplink (the link to the sales page with your Clickbank ID embedded) you will see something like this:

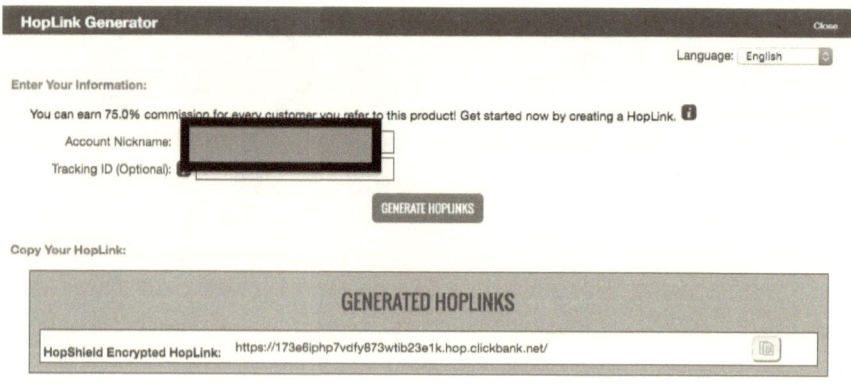

Note that some companies will have multiple links that can be used to visit different pages. In that case, you will have to decide for yourself which page is best to use. On the affiliate page, the company may have instructions on which page converts the best and different options that can be used to your advantage, like offering coupons/discounts to entice a sale. They also may have instructions directly on their affiliate page on how to build your hoplink. You will want to copy and save your hoplink; you are going to use it in multiple ways, as we will see later.

Prettying Up the Link

It can look awkward presenting a link like that to people, obviously, so you can disguise it with text using various programs, but you might also consider visiting tinyurl.com to shorten the link and disguise the clickbank.net reference. The inclusion of the Clickbank link might turn some customers off, but for the most part, the general public doesn't know what Clickbank is.

Looking for high paying products

Most of the products we've looked at so far pay in the $30 range. That isn't bad and you can make a profit on some volume. But it is going to be harder to break even and make a profit given the expenses of driving traffic. Of course, if you are passionate about the subject, you can use free traffic methods to drive traffic to the site, and so any sales obtained are just free money, in the sense of not having to spend on advertising. Now I am not trying to discourage you; it is definitely possible to use paid traffic and make solid profits on a $30 product, but I just want to let you know that there are many higher-paying products.

One area where you are going to find those is in the business opportunity niche. A big money maker online is selling people training on how to make money online! Here, we see one such product – that is the Super Affiliate System by John Crestani. It pays approximately $472 per sale.

Super Affiliate System - John Crestani's Autowebinar Funnel (view mobile)

Avg $/sale

Converts On Cold Bizopp Traffic. 50% Commission. John Crestani's Super Affiliate System & Internet Jetset Group Shows Aspiring Entrepreneurs How To Leverage Paid Traffic To Create An Affiliate Marketing Based Business. High Converting Webinar Funnel.

$472.67

Affiliate Page: https://johncrestani.com/jvs/
Affiliate Support Contact: support@johncrestani.com

Vendor Spotlight

Stats: Initial $/sale: $423.68 | Avg %/sale: 50.0% | Avg Rebill Total: $386.70 | Avg %/rebill: 52.0% | Grav: 52.21
Cat: E-business & E-marketing : Affiliate Marketing

As we mentioned earlier, it is going to take more convincing to get someone to drop $500 than $30. But that also depends on the value being offered as well. Crestani uses a webinar to sell his course, so you can send customers to the webinar signup form. As you can see, his course has a gravity of 52, which is very solid. People ARE selling this product. He also offers a lot with the product, which makes it worth the money. Evaluate high paying products to see what they offer and whether or not it will look worth it to the prospective buyer. People in this niche are going to be willing to pay a lot more money for a product as well – if you are going to start an online business, you are probably willing to lay out $1,000 for training, but you are probably not going to want to spend that much on a diet book.

Believe it or not, there are some products that pay commissions well over $2,000.

Website traffic

I recommend installing Similar Web in your browser. Similar Web will tell you how many visitors per month a website has, and it will show you website traffic over the last six months. This will help you decide whether a given product is worth selling. When I pull up the page for the dog training website, I see that traffic has steadily increased, and they are getting 100,000 visitors per month, which is pretty decent:

You can also see other important information like the Bounce Rate, which tells you how many people visit one page on the site and leave. You can also see various rankings and the estimated duration visitors stay on the site.

Here is what I found for the *Keto Resources* product: It looks better in terms of visitors as compared to the dog training product, but note that they are spending half as much time on the site.

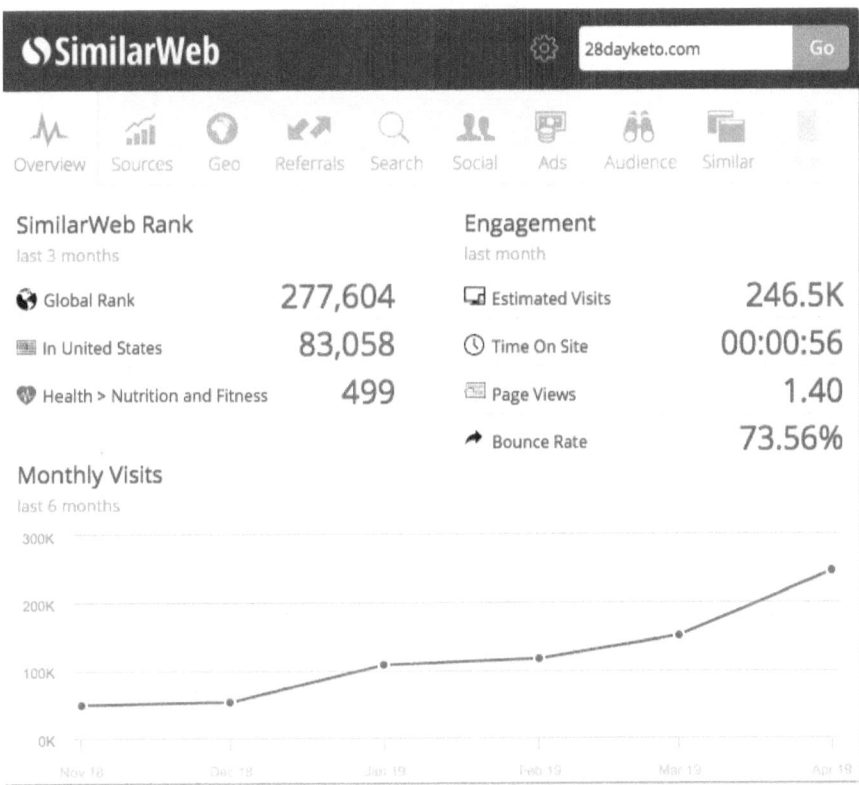

We have to take that with a grain of salt because we don't necessarily know why at this point. People might jump to order right away, or maybe the visitors to the dog site are more hesitant to purchase. Or the opposite – maybe they are more engaged and most visitors to the

Keto site think that it is bogus. Here is what we see from Crestani's super affiliate page:

Similar Web is a tool that you can use in conjunction with other information that is available. It should not be taken to evaluate a product on its own.

What all those symbols mean

You may have noticed that below a Clickbank product, there is a lot of information and several symbols. Let's quickly go over them. The first item you will see at the bottom is one of more flags. This tells you the languages the product is available in. A U.S. flag means English. Other options include French, German, Spanish, Italian, Portuguese, and Spanish.

Next, you will see a green dollar sign or two blue arrows. The green dollar sign means that the product is a one-time sale. The blue arrows mean it's a recurring billing product or subscription. Note that in that case, each month or quarter (whatever the term offered) you will get the sales commission. Next, you might see a small icon that looks like a box that indicates it's a physical product. If you see an orange arrow indicated, that means that the company offers an upsell option. That means that after the customer has purchased the product being offered, they will have the option of spending more money to buy an upgrade or an additional product. Of course, you get the commission for that as well. Finally, there is a wrench and screwdriver icon if they have an Affiliate Tools page.

Stats Section

The stats section provides information about how the product is selling and the money that can be made.

- Initial $/Sale: The average amount of commission you will earn for selling this product.
- Avg Rebill Total: If it is a recurring product (has a subscription), how much you will earn on average.
- Avg $/Sale: This is the total average including initial sale plus rebills if applicable.
- Avg %/Sale: The commission paid as a percentage of the total sale. Most vendors are quite generous.
- Avg %/Rebill: Your commission for rebills as a percentage.
- Grav: The Gravity measure discussed earlier (trademarked by Clickbank).
- Cat: The marketplace category.

CB Graph

A good website to use to evaluate Clickbank products is CBGraph:

http://www.cbgraph.com

You can use this site to find out important information about each product, such as how the gravity of the product changes with time.

Summing Up

So we've explained what a niche is, compared evergreen vs. trending niches, and demonstrated how to pick winning products. We've also shown you some things you will want to look for in a product and what they offer to affiliates. The next step is to drive traffic. There are two basic ways you can do it: Using paid traffic and free/organic traffic.

Chapter 3: Getting Traffic

In this chapter, we will turn to the important topic of getting traffic to your offer. There are many ways you can pitch a product, but the main ways that affiliates use are to create review pages or to create a landing page. Landing pages are signup forms for email lists and they remain the go-to for marketing purposes online. However, review pages are also very effective, and you can use those with pair or free traffic.

Free vs. Paid Traffic

If you don't have money to invest, then "free" traffic may be an option for you. But it is important to realize that nothing is truly free. You will pay for the traffic by having to invest a lot of effort upfront. That is why you should pick a topic that you are interested in to begin with, so that you can enjoy writing making videos about it in the meantime. Some people want you to believe that "free traffic" is likened to a magic pill you can use to get money. The internet is overcrowded and it takes A LOT of work to get your free traffic to bring in visitors.

Free Traffic Ideas

There are several free traffic sources that you can use. These include:

- Creating a blog about the topic of interest
- Answering questions on sites like YahooAnswers and Quora.com
- Contributing to forms across the Internet
- Creating and posting YouTube videos
- Creating a Facebook page
- Other social media

You're not going to use only one of these methods; to be successful in getting the traffic you need, you will have to use all of them. What you are going to do is tie them all together by linking between them to help drive traffic. The purpose of this is because you want to establish a solid online presence. The main goal of doing this is to project yourself as an *authority figure* on the subject matter at hand. Google loves "authority sites".

So the starting point is to create and build a blog. While there are many articles available online, even many for sale for you to use, your blog needs to contain completely original material. So you can see why pursuing free traffic is going to be a lot of work. Frequent creation of posts on the blog is going to be necessary, and it's going to take months to drive traffic. Anyone who tells you otherwise is lying.

With that said, over time, this method will work, and by interlinking between all the various sites, you can make it work faster. The very first step that you must take is to create a blog and establish yourself as knowledgeable on the subject matter.

This is going to require a minimum of 20 feature-length articles. You're going to base each article on a solid keyword that is important for your niche. To find keywords that you can use to create articles with, you can visit either Bing or the Google Keyword Planner.

Google is preferred but either one will do to get a measure of traffic. So jump on Google right now and find their keyword planner. When using it, you are going to use the main phrase or hook to generate long-tail keywords (those may be longer phrases that aren't searched for as much but can help you drive traffic).

One benefit of long-tail keywords there is less competition, and while the audience is smaller, it will give you a chance to get some free eyeballs. When you create an article, you're going to want you to use your keyword in the title, and you also want to use it at least three times in the article, but no more than that.

Google does not like keyword stuffing and they know how to detect it. So you should use the keyword three times – no more, no less. Also, you want to make sure that you are using the keywords in a natural manner. So, don't force the use of the keywords. Use them naturally as you would in conversation.

As an example, the phrase "keto diet", would be a main or hook phrase that you would use to start generating search ideas. The phrase "keto diet" would not be used as an article topic because it's far too broad and the competition is fierce beyond belief. If you base your article solely on that keyword, it's going to end up on page 100 of search and nobody's going to see it.

However, you will want to sprinkle a couple of those popular keywords in your article as well. So in our case, starting with the phrase "keto diet", let's think of some ways that we can find a more long tail keyword that is less popular, to build an article around. One easy way to come up with a long tail keyword that is good for an article topic is to put in something specific about the general keyword. So for example, I could type, "seven ways to overcome digestive problems on the Keto diet". Or you may type in, "Top 10 ways to eat cheap with Keto diets". Lists that include specific numbers (5, 7, or 10, etc.) are great ways to write blog posts and help guide you in creating an article with less thought invested in it.

Another strategy that I have found to be very effective is to visit YouTube and see what popular videos are made on the general topic. So for this example, you could go to YouTube and search the phrase "Keto diet". Then you can see videos that have been made on related topics and use them as headlines for your articles. Of course, don't copy anyone exactly; just use their titles as guidelines and make sure to keep the search phrase exactly as how you have defined it.

Getting Your Blog Ready for Launch

So the first step is to use this process to write 20 articles on your blog. You're going to want to make sure to include at least one picture in each article and have a nice image as the theme at the top of the blog header.

Also, within each article, you should carefully insert links in your blog that point to the sales page of the product that you are trying to sell from Clickbank. The link should be disguised – so for example, instead of putting the Clickbank link for *The Keto Resources* product, I would have the phrase "plan for Keto diet" carefully placed a couple of times in the article, and turn that into a hoplink. When you do that, you use the Clickbank affiliate link for that phrase.

You're going to want to make sure that your blog looks good as well. So you should choose a good theme, and to be blunt, if you're going to go free, it's going to be more difficult. But there are some decent free word press themes that you can use.

Also the Google site blogger.com makes pretty decent looking blogs that you can use. You could also use wordpress.com for the same purpose, but you'll want to check their policy on using affiliate links before you do that. You don't want to get in a situation where you create a blog with a lot of work and have them remove it all of a sudden.

Some people advise that you get your own domain name. That does look more professional. However, unless you're selling your own product, it's not strictly necessary. People are very used to blogs on the Internet, and so having a blog that appears to just be talking about a topic is not going to be controversial in any way or look unprofessional. As far as people know that come across this, they are going to think you're just writing articles. They are not going to be saying to themselves, *Well this person is selling a product; how come it is not a company website?* That is unless you overdo it, so don't oversell in your articles.

You can also use banners if the product vendor on Clickbank provides them and place them on your blog. You can add one on the sidebar and include them once in the middle of your articles. To the visitor of your blog, they are going to look like nothing more than

AdSense ads, which are very common on the Internet anyway. Be sure to link the image with your Clickbank affiliate link. That way, if someone clicks on it, it will take them to the sales page and give you credit for any sales that result.

After you create your blog, one of the most important steps is to make sure that the search engines can find the blog. You're going to want to go to the webmaster tools of at least Google and also probably Bing.com. Sometimes, some web hosts create problems with getting your blog found by the search engines (note that if you create it with blogger.com or wordpress.com this will probably not be a problem, but it might be an issue with your own domain). So you're going to want to make sure that the robot.txt file in your site is set up so all of the search engines can navigate your site. You're also going to want to make sure that you have a mobile-friendly template for your blog, and that you submit your site for indexing. A lot of people say that is not required to submit your site to search engines anymore, but it does help to get it crawled faster. The purpose of this book is not for the technical matters and setting up a website, so I encourage you to do research online to find out how to properly set up your robot.txt file so that the search engines can navigate your blog.

First Steps to Driving Traffic

Once you have your blog set up, and with 20 articles posted to make sure that the first visitor sees the blog as something with substantial content, you can start setting things up so that the traffic is driven to the blog.

There are multiple ways you can do this. The first way that I recommend is to set up a Facebook page on the topic. That's pretty easy to do, so just go to Facebook and click on the "Pages" tab and create a page. You can create the page under your own name if you wish, or you can use a pen name. If you opt for the latter, you can find an image on a stock photo site if you don't want to use your own picture.

Facebook pages are actually kept separate from your personal account, so unless you invite people, your friends and family are not going to see the page. Remember that this is business, so it's up to you how you handle it.

The purpose of setting up a Facebook page is so that you can use the Facebook page to post articles from the blog. That way, you will have backlinks to the blog and also have a presence on Facebook.

You don't want to do it all at once as that will make it look artificial or even spammy. So the first time you create the Facebook page, you can just post the first article you wrote on your blog.

Then you can come back every day and post two or three more articles. You can also use the Facebook page as a place to embed YouTube videos that you have posted if you are doing that as well.

This is not going to be a once-and-done process. To drive free traffic, it is going to require active involvement for some time. So, sadly, after you have the blog set up with 20 articles, you are far from done. You should be writing articles as much as possible. Many experts estimate that it will take a full year to drive free traffic to a blog with any significant quantities. Using some of the techniques here, we are going to speed that up through backlinking, but it still may take several months. So you're going to have to write articles at least three times a week. And if you are serious about this as far as making money, you might try to find one article per day to post. At least three of the articles you post per week should be very substantial in length. So each time you post a new blog post, get the link to the post, and go to your Facebook page and post it there as well.

So if you decide to create other social media accounts, which can only help your cause, you can do the same with them as well. The purpose of the other social media accounts would be to drive more traffic to your blog. So what you can do is to make sure that with each article, you post a nice looking image. Then you can create an Instagram account for the business, and then post your articles on Instagram.

You can also create a Twitter account and do the same so you create a tweet with a link back to your blog article. You may try including links to your articles in comments that you post on related Twitter accounts, in Facebook groups, or articles that you find on social media accounts. Just don't make it look like spam. Be sure to post some relevant comments and then leave a link back to your article at the end of the comment.

Using Q&A Sites Like Quora

Quora is an excellent site that you can use to help drive not only traffic but backlinks to your blog. Generating backlinks is an important tool that can be used to help improve your ranking in the search engines. So the way that you use this site, is that you look for questions related to the topic of your blog. This is not very hard at all for popular topics like the Keto diet.

So you're going to go on Quora and then you look for people that are asking questions about the Keto diet, for example. Then post an answer to the person's question, and then at the end of the question leave a link back to your article on your blog. You can even look for questions and then write articles on your blog in response to link back to.

It's important to note that the staff on Quora are looking for spammers posting affiliate links. So you have to be very careful about doing this. But if you follow the steps I'm going to tell you right now, it's going to work. The first step is to provide a *substantial* answer. So don't answer someone's question with a one-liner. Put some thought into it and put two or three paragraphs.

Then you want to have an article on your blog, which is directly related to the question in some way. If you post unrelated links, the staff may flag your account and possibly ban you from the site.

However, if you post *related* articles from your blog that are relevant, they will allow them to stay up. The backlink to your blog from the Quora site is going to be very valuable and helping your blog move up in the search engines, and it's also going to provide you free traffic from Quora for many months and even years to come.

Before you go about doing this, make sure that your blog is totally set up to drive traffic to the Clickbank sales page. So make sure to have a banner or two, and some links within the article.

Email Signup Forms

Also, you're going to want to have an email sign-up form on your website. Probably the best way to do it in this example is to have a pop-up window - you have probably seen many of them and frankly, they are annoying - it's a small form that lets people sign up to join your email list. Often they show up when someone moves the mouse to leave the page.

We are going to talk about setting up an email list later, but it's a vital step to online marketing. You don't want people just visiting your blog and then disappear forever. If they were interested enough to look, what you want to do is capture their email so you can sell to them.

YouTube Reviews

So one strategy that is very commonly used is to review a product on YouTube, and then link it to the Clickbank product with your affiliate link in the description of the video, or possibly a link to a related article on your blog or a landing page. In order for the strategy to work, you have to be halfway-decent and make videos. However, that doesn't mean that you have to be some kind of actor or have the star power or be the best-looking person in the world. All you have to do is record yourself with your smart phone talking about the product. Or you can show previews of the product on screen and use a screen recording software product to make the video.

Again, it doesn't have to be great – you can shoot yourself talking in your living room or you can record yourself in front of the computer with a WebCam. Just talk for a few minutes about the product and how it's helped you. And then you can drive people toward either some kind of review page, lead page, or sales page for the product. YouTube is one place where you can directly link to the sales page of the vendor with your hoplink.

If you're going to put up YouTube videos, I recommend that you install a free product called VideoIQ. This product analyzes other YouTube videos and will tell you what keywords they are using for tags on their videos to help drive search. That is important to help your video get views. So, look at a similar topic that is made into a video on YouTube and see what tags they are using and also note the title of their video.

Obviously, you don't want to copy anyone directly, but use that as a guideline. After you post your YouTube video, then you can post a blog post that has the YouTube video in it. Then after that, go to

Facebook and post the YouTube video there on your Facebook page. You can also include the YouTube video, if it's not too cheesy, in forums and places like that as well.

Forum Posting

So this brings us to the next topic, which is posting in forums. Essentially, this is no different than posting on Quora.com. So are you going to try and find popular forums that address your topic? It's important to note that many of the moderators of these forums despise affiliate marketers. So the last thing you want to do is directly link back to an affiliate product.

In all cases, whether it's on the forum, or on Quora.com or YahooAnswers.com, what you want to do is to add value to the conversation. As long as you're adding value, your post is not likely to be deleted. To add value in your comments, and instead of linking directly to the sales page of the product, link back to a relevant article on your blog. And be sure to have a pop-up email sign-up form set up on your blog so that when people go there, you can capture their email address and then you can sell to them in future. Of course, hopefully, some will click on a banner or something on your website and you'll get a sale straightaway.

So the strategy that I have outlined here to drive free traffic will definitely work. At least I will say it will work if you post quality material. However, this type of strategy will take time so it is only of use to the patient ones amongst us. You must give the strategy several months to work, and you must keep posting regularly in order for it to work. The search engines are going to be monitoring the amount of content on your site, whether or not it's original content, and how frequently the website is updated. Google loves so-called "authority" websites. By studying your subject and routinely posting on your blog, you can establish it as an authority website and a favorite in Google and other search engines.

A Review Site

No, I'm going to discuss an alternative free traffic strategy. You can use some of the techniques used in the last section to help drive traffic for this strategy, but this is more of a static-type strategy. In order to do this rather than set up a blog, you're going to set up a website with multiple pages. This can be a set-it-and-forget-it website, where you only post new reviews as new related-Clickbank products go on the market.

You are going to review multiple affiliate marketing products on this website that all belong to the same niche. So what you could do, for example, is create a website to review weight loss products. In order to make it look a little bit more authentic, you might wish to write some reviews of general diets that people are currently trying besides just reviewing Clickbank products. So you can include a review of Jenny Craig, Weight Watchers, the Atkins diet, etc.

Then over time, you could add reviews of specific weight-loss products that are for sale on Clickbank. So with this strategy, rather than just promoting one product, you're going to promote multiple products for a given niche and write one webpage for each product. The review should be as sincere as possible. The review should also not be just a couple of paragraphs. The web favors content. So you don't want it so lengthy that readers are bored to death, but it should be a few pages long. This sounds like a lot of work but if you want free traffic, there is no other way. If the vendor has pictures, and so forth, from their affiliate page such as pictures of the books, software discs, and so forth, include those pictures in your article.
You want your article to look nice and appealing in addition to having good content.

As far as tone goes, you're going to recommend the product, but try to make it as sincere a review as possible. If it's available, you're going to want to request a review copy of the product from the vendor. Some vendors will offer them and others will not – you just have to ask. However, if you can get a review copy and actually go through the product, you're going to be able to write a real review which will carry a lot more weight.

Whether or not a site like this requires constant activity or not, that's not really the same as a blog, so it's unclear. However, are you still going to want some substantial content to include at least 20 review articles? Of course, it is really going to help if you can find 20 or more products of the same niche on Clickbank and review them all on the same website – it might help you drive in some free traffic that pays off.

Here is an example of this type of site:

http://www.healthyweightforum.org/eng/diets/2-week-diet/

Depending on how much time and effort you want to put into this, keep in mind that these different methods are not mutually exclusive. So you can set up a blog and the Facebook page and everything that we described above, and then you can set up a separate website that reviews different Clickbank products.

There is no reason not to have both, and the more substantial presence you have online, the more traffic that you're going to be driving, possibly leading to sales.

So you might ask how often you should post on sites like Quora.com. The answer is: As often as possible but not too much to make you look like some kind of spammer. So a good example might be to post once per day or 3 to 5 times per week. Of course, you're not going rely on one site; you're going to want to find a few related forums or even newspaper articles where you can make posts. Of course, you need to be aware that not everyone is going to allow you to post the link back to your blog, but you're just going to have to use trial and error to find places that will allow it.

Paid Traffic

In this section, we are going to talk about using paid traffic. Right now, by far the number one source of paid traffic is using Facebook ads. If possible, you want to see if you can get a lookalike audience from the product vendor. If that's possible, you're going to be able to make a lot of conversions. Your ad should link back to a squeeze page or email sign-up form. Here is an example:

Facebook ads are reviewed by real people, and they are relatively strict. Some different products like business opportunities or "Start an Online Business" trainings are not allowed on Facebook. And if you're going to use diet products, you're going to have to be a little bit careful about what you say in your ad and on the page the ad directs traffic to. Don't make outlandish claims in your ad or on your squeeze page.

Now, if a lookalike audience is not available, then you're going to have to do regular Facebook advertising and build up an audience over time. The way you'll do this is to try to find interests that the audience has that is related to your product. So if you are selling a Keto diet product, you're going to want to look for people on Facebook who have liked pages related to weight loss or dieting.

You'll put this in your ad to refine your audience and I recommend that you either drive people to your email sign-up form or create a Facebook-likes campaign for your Facebook page. A Facebook page has to be attached to any type of ad campaign you run on Facebook.

So obviously before you do this, you're going to want to put 20 links back to your blog on your Facebook page so that when people like your page during the ad campaign, they're going to see something that they can read and looks substantial rather than something new and fly-by-night.

When someone likes your page, every time you post on it, it's going to appear on *their* Facebook feed. Be sure to treat that with respect. In other words, you should spend most of your time posting relevant content that people find interesting about the topic. As always, you can subtly link back to the affiliate product in your articles.

After you build up a large number of likes and so have an audience that you can post to regularly, once in a while, you can post an offer. But don't do it very often as you don't want to appear to be a pushy salesman.

As far as ad spend, start off small and build up. You don't want to be spending hundreds of dollars on Facebook right away especially if you're going to find out that your ad doesn't work very well. To begin with, a five-dollar-a-day ad suffices, and if your ad seems to convert well, slowly raise it by a dollar or so a day until you get to a budget that you are comfortable with, and you're driving a reasonable amount of traffic. If it doesn't seem to convert very well, then try new images, videos or copy and then relaunch it.

Solo Ads

The second type of ad that we are going to talk about is called a *solo ad*. Solo advertising is basically leveraging on somebody else's email list. This is a very important and very useful method of advertising online products. One website you can check out is called Udimi.com, and you can find others by searching for the phrase *solo ads*.

So what happens with the solo ad is that there are people that sell access to their email list. So they may have a list of thousands, tens of thousands, or even more than 100,000 customers. So you can buy however many clicks you want that would drive from their list to your lead page where you can get these people to sign up on your email list. The nice thing about solo ads is that there are no restrictions on what you can advertise.

So things that you can't advertise on Facebook, you can advertise on solo ads such as business opportunities or start your own Internet business. The way it works is that the person that owns the list will send out an email to their list on your behalf pitching your webpage.

Then some of their users will sign off on your form. It's done by a number of clicks basis, so they will generate 100 clicks or 1,000 clicks to your web page as you pay and agree to. Not all will sign up, but since these are typically hot email lists of people that buy online, you might get 20-30% of the people to sign up to join your email list.

Start small and find a good advertiser before jumping in and spending hundreds of dollars. Not all people selling solo ads are created equal. Some are fraudsters that will sell fake bot traffic, so you need to be aware of that.

But if you stick to a reliable site like Udimi.com, that will help weed out most of the fraudsters, and you can read reviews about the particular sellers too.

This method of advertising is very useful, it's not very expensive, and it can be very productive. Start off by doing 100 at clicks at a time. Honestly, I prefer it to Facebook. No hassle and nobody looking over your shoulder making judgments about what you're selling.

PPC Ads

Another method that has been as old as the web itself is pay-per-click (PPC) advertising. You create a short text ad that appears in a search engine like Google or Bing, and you pay for clicks to lead to your website. You can use this to generate traffic to a lead page or a review page on your website. The more expensive the product you are pitching, the more PPC is worth it. It is not as successful for lower-priced products. Unfortunately, in recent years, Google has gotten quite expensive.

So many people are staying away from it now unless they've got pretty deep pockets. However, Bing.com is not nearly as expensive and you can still reach out to millions of people with it. Just keep in mind that, as with Facebook, these companies have attitudes about certain types of products and you may not be able to advertise them on there. You also often have to stick to linking back to lead pages to avoid too much controversy – but that's OK because you want to get people on your mailing list anyway.

YouTube

Making video ads are turning into one of the leading ways to drive paid traffic to websites without spending a lot of money. You need to have a video uploaded to your YouTube account in order to do this.

Then, create an advertising account to associate with the YouTube account. You can then create a campaign, select the video and then pick who you want to see it, including countries and even specific YouTube channels or videos.

So what should you put in your video? The best kind of video to use is you talking about the product or issues in which the product solves. It doesn't have to be very long or fancy – a couple of minutes will do. You are just trying to get people to click on your landing page, so that you can talk about the freebie they will get for signing up on your landing page.

If possible, see if the vendor of the product you are promoting has a video that they will allow you to use.
Compared to PPC, YouTube advertising is dirt cheap.

If you aren't sure what kind of video to make, the best thing to do is get on YouTube and watch videos in your niche, and see what kinds of ads other people are making.

Chapter 4: Setting Up an Email List

In this chapter, we're going to talk about the all-important email list. For many years, an email list has been a vital complement to every online marketer's toolkit. One of the main reasons that you're going to want an email list is that people have some natural skepticism the first time they are exposed to a product.

So, the very first time someone sees a review or lands on the sales page, most people are not going to simply pull out their credit cards. However, an email list provides you with a way to directly communicate with the prospects and to build up a relationship with your potential customer. So you are going to want to provide some value in your emails.

You do this by talking to them about the topics of interest in your niche. This has the purpose of getting the customer to begin to see you as a trusted person. And then, when you recommend to them that they purchase the product, they are going to trust your judgment because you have provided value to them in the emails. Many of them will actually buy the product at that point. This is a very effective way of marketing.

It also adds extra value. In other words, once you have people on your email list, you can sell to them again and again as the months go by. So what you can do is, over time, you can pitch related products to people on your email list. Suppose that if we created an email list for Keto dieters, in six months, if some other product came out, we could still safely assume that some people on the list have not reached their weight loss goals. Therefore, we could pitch the new product to them. Or if some Keto-related product came out, we can always pitch that new idea to the mailing list.

Setting all this up honestly sounds like a lot of work – but many services will automatically do this for you.

Probably the top service is either Aweber.com or GetResponse. There are also some others such as Mailchimp. Check these out and pick the one that you like best. Aweber is tops, but they all do basically about the same thing. GetResponse is nice in that you have a graphical/node kind of setup where you can plan out your email sequences.

So what you want to do is to set up an automated responder inside the service that you select. This is nothing more than a series of emails arranged to be sent on specific days, starting from the first day that they sign up to join your list.

So if you're using Aweber, for example, what you do is you go in there and create a list for your topic. After you have completed that step, then you create your first email message and add it to the list, to be sent automatically when the person signs on. From there, you create a legacy follow-up series that contains multiple emails. The idea is that, when I first sign up for your list, you send me an email immediately.

Then you send me a series of emails over the course of the next couple of weeks or a month, or even several months if you desire to do this. You may send me emails as many times as you want.

In the beginning, when the customer is a hot prospect, you should send them a lot of emails in a row. Now you don't want to send more than one per day, but the first couple of days you might send two or three in a row, and then after that, skip a day and start again the day after that. You can start sending them emails every other day or so instead of daily to slow it down.

Then as time goes on, gradually lengthen the time in between emails until maybe you're sending out one a week or one every month. If you're planning to do this for the long term, and stay in the niche for the long term, you might want to send emails on a regular basis.

You can also do what's called a "broadcast", which is an email that you can compose for a one-time send out to your list. So if you have a long-term list that you're building on a certain niche like weight loss, you can use a broadcast message to send them information about new weight-loss products that come out. The larger the list you have, the more money you can make from the list. People on an email list are generally far more responsive than the general public. So while you may normally only get 1% of traffic to a sales page that buy the product, from an email list, you might be able to get 10% of them to buy it.

So let's talk about how to structure your emails. The first email is not going to be used for a hard sell. What you want to do in the first email is to provide a lot of value to your potential client. So you should pick a topic to talk about that will be of interest to your email subscriber. And spend three or four paragraphs simply talking about the topic without offering any kind of product.

So, for example, if we were doing the ketogenic diet, in the first email you could write three or four paragraphs on what foods are banned from the ketogenic diet. So this will be something that is informative to a beginner on a ketogenic diet. Or as another example, you could explain to them what insulin is and how it works with the ketogenic diet. Then after providing, say, three paragraphs worth of content, you can briefly recommend the affiliate products towards the end of your email. Using *The Keto Resources* as an example, their idea is a 30-day plan for the diet, so you could say, "Here I have found a product which lays out a plan that lasts a month for you to try – the Keto diet, and they tell you exactly what to eat". But you don't want to be hard selling in your first email, keep that in mind. Otherwise, they will be reluctant to open the second and subsequent emails.

So you can send the second email right away and that means send it the following day. Don't send more than one email per day, as I'm not even sure that some of the services allow that. So on the second day, you also want to provide a lot of valuable content. So figure out another topic of interest to the reader that you can discuss in a friendly tone. This time you might want to write a couple of paragraphs, and then find some way to recommend the product in the middle of your email. But make sure that it's relevant in some way to what was talked about in the paragraph above it.

Then add on another couple paragraphs of content. Toward the end, just as you're going to sign off on the email, recommend the product again with your affiliate link a second time.

Some people also like to add a "P.S." at the end of their email where they recommend the product with the link again. One thing that has been found about marketing online is that you need to provide opportunities for the customer to take action and buy the product. So you don't want to be shy about putting links to the affiliate product in your emails and putting more than one so that they can find it and click on it to buy the product. It's all a matter of balance.

After this, you might want to skip one day. Then come back with another informative email on a third topic. Again, you can sprinkle links to your affiliate product in the email. The following day, you can try doing a hard sell. So this time, sending an email directly appeals to the reader that they should buy the product and you may put a link to buy the product. After this, skip a day and then on the following day, come back with an informative email, and you can even leave off the affiliate link altogether. Later on, you can send more emails that include the affiliate link. You can also use your email series to pitch other related products to your clients.

So, for example, if you look on Clickbank, you can find Keto diet products that pitch making bread, desserts or cookbooks that are keto-friendly. So you can offer these to a list of keto-interested buyers. So of course, in the end, we are going to need some way to get people to sign up. And the way to do that is to create a "squeeze" page or a landing page (same thing), but before we do that, we need to create or give them access to some kind of free giveaway – that can be a book or video used as a bribe to get buyers to sign up for your list. So we're going to discuss that in the next chapter before we talk about squeeze pages.

Chapter 5: How to Create a Giveaway or Freebie

In order to get people to join your email list, you want to offer them some type of freebie in exchange for joining the list. This can be a book in the form of a downloadable PDF, or a training video of interest. So you will want to set up a web page that makes the offer in exchange for them signing up. You can call this a bribe if you want – that is a fair characterization.

Hopefully, the vendor of the product you are trying to sell has giveaway products that you can use to get people onto your list. However, the sad reality is that while many do, most vendors don't offer giveaways for you. So you are going to have to figure out ways you can create or obtain your own giveaway, which we are going to talk about in this chapter. Even if you have someone else write one for you, it's good to know about the structure of the document which you should try to emulate.

It is important to make sure that at some point in the document, you have your affiliate link.

Buying a Giveaway

There are sources of giveaway documents that you can utilize. These are called Private Label Rights (PLR) or Master Resale Rights products. These are digital products that someone else is selling that you can use in your own business. A good place to look for resources is the PLR Store. Find it at:

http://www.theplrstore.com

You can browse here for relatively inexpensive PDF guides that have been written by an expert in the field. They are not going to be as good as the products that are being sold on Clickbank by a long shot, but they are good enough to give away for free in order to entice users to sign up and join your email list.

Not all guides can be given away for free. Be sure to review the legal restrictions for each guide. Normally, they come with a PDF and Word version of the document. You are going to have to edit the Word version and insert your affiliate link for the Clickbank product in the document.

Hiring an Expert on Fiverr

Now, you might want to put "expert" in quotes. However, Fiverr can be a useful place to hire a writer. Chances are, you are going to end up with someone from India or the Philippines, but that is fine because many of these people are very well educated and speak English well, but you are going to want to check them out for this purpose first. The best thing to do is request samples of previous work so you can vet them for quality. Then, you can send them an outline for the document. They will be expected to research the topic on their own and then write a readable guide. Only accept Microsoft Word format documents so that you can edit the contents as necessary, and before you export the finished product, add your affiliate links to the document. The document should have nice professional formatting with graphics and images. The length should be about 20 pages.

Contents

The main purpose of the document, besides offering a freebie, is to possibly close a sale. The structure should go like this:

- Start with an opportunity (i.e., For the first time, the Keto diet is leading many to lose weight) – 5-6 paragraphs

- State the problem the person in your niche is having (can't lose weight; tried and failed many diets) – 6-8 paragraphs
- Relate this to yourself to create bonding
- Explain how you discovered a solution – 5-6 paragraphs
- The solution happens to be the affiliate product
- Put links to buy the affiliate product at the end of the document

Before you enter the "state the problem" section, you should take an upbeat, excited tone.

Hi, my name is …

I'm thrilled to be here today to tell you about my experiences with the ketogenic diet! Over the past 3 months, I've managed to lose 17 pounds, and now have a trim and fit waistline. I have also beaten back my diabetes!

My blood sugar dropped from 134 to 110 points in the first six weeks of following this diet.

Throughout the document, when you have a chance, introduce a "but… then" section, where you introduce some objection and then propose the product as the solution.

Many new Keto dieters get the "keto flu" and don't know how to proceed. Many end up giving up. That's why I found the <u>28-day Keto plan</u> so helpful. It gave me step-by-step instructions, telling me exactly what to eat to get rid of the keto flu.

==> **Click Here for more info on the 28-Day Keto Plan** <==

Here, the underlined text and the text between the arrows would be the hoplinks to the affiliate product.

You should provide several opportunities for the reader to link to the affiliate product, but don't overdo it. In a 15-page guide, put about 2-3 links. Make sure 2 of the links are on the last 2 pages.

Your Giveaway Item Isn't everything

Your email list is going to be where you do most of your selling, so don't look at the guide as the be-all and end-all. It is an opportunity to sell to the customer, however, so do that. But make most of it valuable content so that they will be glad to have signed up for your email list. You want to prime the readers so that they will be interested in reading the emails that you send them.

Chapter 6: Using Landing Pages/Squeeze Pages to Build an Email List

As we've noted, one of the most important parts of online marketing is to create an email list. The tool used to do that is to set up a landing page. This is a simple 2-page website that is designed for one purpose – to capture the email address of a potential lead so that you can add them to your email list and sell products to them. The landing page is very simple, and typically consists of a background image, headline text, and an email signup form. The text will offer the free guide or other freebies that the customer gets in exchange for filling out the email signup form. When they fill out the form, then you give them access to the free guide on a "thank you" page. The thank you page can also give them a chance to visit the sales page directly and purchase the product immediately. Often, I set up a video about the product on the thank you page with a "call-to-action" button just below the video.

The landing page will be directly integrated with your email auto responder, be it Aweber, Mailchimp, GetResponse or some other service. When the customer clicks on the "submit" button, they will be added to your list automatically.

Historically, services like Aweber have recommended that you use a "double opt-in". What this means is that when someone signs up for your email list, Aweber will send them a confirmation email that asks them if they want to join the list. It is an extra layer of protection to protect people against spam. One thing to note, however, is that if you are going to be using solo ads, turn off the double opt-in feature. Oftentimes, the opt-in mail from Aweber or whatever service you are using ends up in people's spam folders and they never see the message and confirm. If you are using solo ads, shut it off and then when they sign up, your first email automatically gets delivered to them. If you are running Facebook ads, you should keep double opt-ins turned on.

Landing Page Example

Here is an example of a landing page which I've used with solo ads. It's a software product available for affiliates to sell on Clickbank. The basic ideas of a landing page are all there. It has a picture of the software box (even though it is an online product), a message for the prospective buyer and a signup button. When they click on the button, it brings up a popup form that they can use to sign up for my email list:

FREE Video Reveals:
Who Else Wants a Powerful, Proven MT4 Indicator That Generates Super Accurate BUY and SELL Signals So That Even Beginners Can Generate Massive FOREX Profits?

Watch the Free Video to Learn How FOREX MILLENNIUM Can Take Your Trading to the Next Level!

WATCH NOW

Structuring Your Headline

The headline and text that you include on the page are obviously going to be important. It is not that hard to get people to sign up for free stuff, so not much text has to be provided. In this case, I am telling them they get to watch a free video if they sign up for my email list, so that is why I put "WATCH NOW" as the call-to-action button. If you are offering a PDF book for them to download, simply put "DOWNLOAD NOW".

The headline has to entice them to sign up. Many famous marketers stick to a few phrases that are known to reel people in. You can start your headline with:

⇨   Who Else Wants
⇨   Discover
⇨   This Secret Reveals

So you use a sentence structure that starts with the phrase, then make the offer and state a couple of points. You can then add a time limit if desired, with a guarantee. Here is an example:

"Discover how expert traders make huge profits trading options, no matter which way the market moves, doubling their money in 14 days or less, Guaranteed!"

Keep in mind that if you are doing solo ads, you can get outlandish like this. If you are advertising on Facebook, Google, or Bing, however, then you need to be a little more guarded. They do review your pages and they don't like aggressive marketing.

Thank You Page

On the thank you page, I offer the prospect an opportunity right then and there and thank them for signing up. I am not necessarily expecting them to buy immediately – that is what the email newsletter is for. But you may as well give them the opportunity. You can also either provide a download link for the free book you promised or give them an opportunity to watch the video that you offered. In my example, my thank you page looks like this:

The top banner is also a link to the sales page for the product.

Another approach is to have a review article on your thank you page. I took that approach here:

Thanks for signing up for our newsletter! Please check your inbox!

What is the Custom Keto Diet?

The Custom Keto Diet is a step-by-step information-packed ketogenic diet plan developed just for you. Everyone is different and you'll get a plan complete with shopping lists and meal ideas developed for your age, gender, activity level, and more. Each plan includes only food groups you specify in your preferences, which can be modified at any time.

Get your Custom Keto Plan Here

What Do You Get With the Custom Keto Diet?

How to Get Your Pages Made

There are many different ways that you can get your landing pages all set up. The old fashioned and the most difficult way is to create your own website and then add these kinds of pages to it, perhaps building them up manually or having a coder create them for you. But those days have long gone. There are many services that allow you to create squeeze pages (or, interchangeably, landing pages). Some of the top sites that let you do this are:

⇨ Instapage

⇨ Leadpages

⇨ ClickFunnels

Quite frankly, ClickFunnels is the only option that you should consider. Leadpages and Instapage aren't bad, and they are older services that have been around for awhile. But ClickFunnels is amazing. First of all, it is extremely user-friendly and powerful. You can design all of the pages you want to include in what they call a "sales funnel" using drag-and-drop capabilities, and include anything on them like videos, links, images, and buttons.

But one thing about ClickFunnels is the fact that it was designed by one of the world's leading internet marketers, a fellow named Russell

Brunson. He cut his teeth moving from nobody to become a world-leading marketer, so he KNOWS how this business works and that really comes through with ClickFunnels the way it does, not with the other services which now seem shabby by comparison. Moreover, ClickFunnels has a lot of the in-built functions that you might need to run your business. You can create domain names inside of it and even create email auto responders. It integrates with virtually every website service you will need for your business. Even though it has the capability of creating its own email auto responder sequence built-in right there, I prefer to use the older services like Aweber and Mailchimp to take care of my lists. They are easily integrated into ClickFunnels.

What is a Sales Funnel?

So, gone are the days of websites. Welcome to the world of sales funnels. If you are going to strictly run on paid traffic, although you can include a blog or review site as we discussed earlier, as an affiliate marketer, you can simply build a sales funnel in a service like ClickFunnels, and that is all you will ever need.

A sales funnel is simply a series of steps designed to close a prospect. The first step of any sales funnel is going to be the lead page, or the sales page built to collect email addresses. A sales funnel can have only a couple of steps or it can have several steps. What you can do is to track people who are actually opening your emails, and send them to different steps in your funnel. The end game of the funnel is to close your sale, of course.

For beginning affiliate marketers, you are generally going to have very simple sales funnels. Product vendors, especially when they are selling high ticket items, are going to want more complicated sales funnels. But if you are selling smaller products off Clickbank, then you will need a lead page, a thank you page, and perhaps a review page where you post your own personal review of the product.

A video review of the product can be pretty effective in particular, and you might want to post that on YouTube and then use that in your funnel step on ClickFunnels.

Chapter 7: Common Mistakes

In this chapter, we're going to talk about common mistakes that are made by beginning affiliate marketers. Obviously, it's not as easy as it sounds or everyone will be running around with $1 million in their pocket. So there are many mistakes that are commonly made that lead potential affiliate marketers to fail very early on and never make any money at all. So let's have a look at some of the more common mistakes.

Sending Traffic Directly to Sales Pages

The first mistake that affiliate marketers make is that they try to drive traffic directly to the sales page of the vendor on Clickbank. They can do this in a myriad of ways but one of the most common ways the people try to do is to open up Google AdWords or a Bing Advertising Account and create a PPC ad that goes *directly* to the sales page. Now it's possible that you could write really good copy in your pay-per-click ad and get lucky and make a few sales. In the early days of the Internet, this technique actually worked pretty well.

But back then, people were kind of starry-eyed getting online and they were eager to buy things immediately and didn't have their skeptic's hat on. Unfortunately for those of us who want to do affiliate marketing today, most people now are very skeptical about buying something online. Of course, that's not true if you're going to Amazon or something like that, but if they see an ad for a weight-loss product as we noted earlier, they are not going to be sitting there pulling their credit card out of their wallet right away.

So the old method of having a simple two-line ad that ran in Google searches back then doesn't work very well anymore. People who try this tactic end up flushing a lot of money down the toilet, in most cases. The problem is that if you are selling a low-dollar item, chances are the one or two sales you might get are not going to make up for the money that you spent on advertising. On the other hand, if you are selling a high-dollar item, there's no way that you're going to sell someone just based on a three-line PPC ad. For high-dollar items, someone is going to need a lot more of what they call pre-selling, which is what we were doing when creating our email list or using/making a review page.

Not Collecting Email Leads

The previous example is actually two mistakes rolled into one. As we described from the last paragraph, the first mistake is that you're not warming up your prospects to make a sale. You're simply sending what they call "cold traffic" to the sales page. And again, that might seem to work a little bit some of the time, but it is not the way the professional marketers work in the space.

So what is the second mistake? The second mistake is that you've lost the customer. Remember, we spent a great deal of time in the book talking about collecting email addresses. The bottom line is you want to be able to be in direct contact with the prospect because you're going to need to spend some time selling to most of them that are going to buy the product.

Also, you may want to keep these people's contact information on hand, so that you can sell more stuff to them later on. So when we collect the name of a prospect using a landing page, we are not just collecting them for the sake of selling them one Clickbank product. You collect the name of the person with their email address so that you can sell them more than one item, and possibly multiple products over an extended period of time. This is the way to dramatically increase your income. So if you were doing pay-per-click traffic and simply sending people straight to the vendors' sales page, they may or may not buy the product. And you would have lost the contact information that the person might have been willing to give to you.

Spending Too Much on Advertising Early

Mistake number three can be described as being overly optimistic. Many people jump in and get really excited and spend far too much money on advertising. People can be anxious about making money and this is understandable. So you might sign up for a Facebook ad, and hope to just drive a huge amount of traffic over a short time period and earn some money quickly. Or you might sign up for a solo ad and buy 1000 clicks. These are huge mistakes that can cost people a lot of money. For example, considering solo ads, you really don't know whether the seller of the ad is legitimate or not until you try it out. So the best thing to do is to spend a small amount of money to get 100 clicks so that you can determine whether or not they're sending you relevant traffic from real people or what not. If they are sending traffic that isn't going to convert for you, this is simply a waste of money.

On the other hand, of course, if you get a lot of people signing up or even get a few sales, then you know that's a good person to do business with in the future. So the problem is that a lot of beginners are eagerly hoping to make big bucks fast and easy, and they go and spend thousands of dollars on ads and they end up with nothing. So you need to take it slow, and as we advised for Facebook ads, start off with five dollars a day and see what happens and then go from there.

Not Carefully Looking at All Stats For a Product

So let's move on to our next mistake. This time, we're going to talk about people that don't carefully evaluate the products that they are trying to sell. The first mistake you can make in this case - and yes there are multiple mistakes you can make - is that you pick a product that has low gravity. Some people either ignore gravity, or they think to themselves that they alone are capable of moving a product that nobody else can.

Another mistake that people can make which we have touched on before is getting a product that has a very high gravity – say over 100. So what happens, in this case, is that a beginning marketer really isn't sure what they're doing and tries to compete with hundreds of Clickbank veterans who are advertising all over the place and pushing up the cost related to that specific product. And although it's selling well, the beginning affiliate marketer can't make any headway.

So although you may be confident, don't overestimate your abilities until you have proven yourself in the marketplace. It's best to get your feet wet with a moderately-selling product instead of trying to duke it out with tons of competition on something that's really popular at the moment. You should also remember that many products that have a very high gravity are in a fad stage and the interest in them may drop down soon.

On the other hand, there are many products with a gravity of between 20 and 50 which are long-term evergreen products. So they aren't selling as fast, but they do provide a solid opportunity to make income without you having to make yourself heard in the noise of hundreds of people promoting the same product. To illustrate this, I suggest that you look up *"red tea detox"* on Clickbank. I want to say I don't have anything against the product per se, but you will notice that it has a very high gravity. And if you start looking up the topic, you are also going to notice that there are tons of people trying to sell this product. All of a sudden you are going to see *red tea detox* all over the place. So the odds of you being able to make a living out of it, may not be as high as they would be in for something that doesn't have overwhelming competition. I do want to say that that doesn't mean you cannot make money selling something like *red tea detox* – you most certainly can. It's just going to be harder to stand out amongst the crowd when you are new to this, and I am not sure that a beginner should be taking that approach.

Expecting Too Much Out of Passive Income

Another mistake is what I call the "set it and forget it" mentality. Let's face it; one of the selling points of online marketing is the idea of passive income. So people are enticed by the possibility that all they have to do is put up one web page and then let the money roll in. And guess what? It doesn't happen like this. So while you can get a passive income from an online affiliate business, it takes a lot of upfront hard work. I hope that I have made that clear in this book.

So you do need to put in the work no matter what you're doing, say creating a blog, making nice landing pages, or whatever, and once everything is rolling, then you're going to have passive income at that point. But keep in mind that even then, it may not be sustainable for the very long term. The reality is that the online world is very fast-moving and always changing. So you might set up a system for passive income and then find that six months from now, it doesn't work anymore.

Relying On One Traffic Source

Another mistake that is commonly made by beginners is trying to rely on only one channel for traffic. So you might think that you can set up a landing page, and then run your business based on Facebook ads. Of course, you might get some traffic, but you're leaving a lot of money on the table. So you should be approaching this by pursuing multiple streams of traffic. That means you should be also advertising using solo ads, or at the very least, YouTube videos, having a blog, and so forth – basically every avenue to get traffic that we have discussed in this book. So here's the next mistake we're going to consider:

Spamming

The next mistake we're going to consider is the type of mistake that leads you to get banned from many websites. For example, a lot of people think, *well it would be easy to place free ads on Craigslist.* So they try to advertise a product on there and then suddenly find that they are banned from Craigslist. Guess what? Although in the early days, it was possible to advertise on Craigslist, it's impossible now. So there are a lot of ways that you can get banned from various sites. For example, you can get banned from Facebook ads if you try to advertise the wrong kind of product that they don't like. Earlier on, we talked a little bit about John Crestoni's Super Affiliate Program. You might not be surprised that Facebook doesn't care for this product at all. Even though it's a legitimate product, Facebook is going to ride you very hard if you try to advertise it on there. And if you push it, they might end up closing down your account. Other ways to have the administrators close your account include spamming message boards and forms, trying to post links where they are not allowed, and posting direct affiliate links rather than going with a link back to your blog or some page that appears harmless. It's always important when you're contributing to forums that you add value to the forum. So you shouldn't just post in the hopes of having a sale; post to enjoy and join in on the conversations. Leave your links back to your blog as an afterthought. When you take this approach, you're more assured that your information will stay up on the website and drive free traffic to you over time.

Expecting Immediate Results

The next mistake is expecting instant results. Affiliate marketing is a lot easier than other types of businesses in many ways. You don't have to keep any inventory, run a store, and all that. You don't even have to interact directly with your customers. However, at the end of it, affiliate marketing is a real business. Most real businesses never work out, and starting a real business is never easy. So, of course, I want to encourage you to use affiliate marketing to make money from home. And you can even grow it into a very large business. However, for most of us, even getting tips like we're giving here, is not going to be easy and it's not going to produce instant results. In the beginning, you should set your goals modestly. If your expectations are not too outlandish, you will be more likely to strive on to keep going and reach certain reachable heights.

Chapter 8: Cross-Selling

In this chapter, we are going to talk about a powerful way to increase your income and that is called "cross-selling". Of course, you have noticed that when we look at a product on Clickbank in a given niche, there are many different products that are related to the same general interest. For example sticking to the Keto diet, you could start off by selling the *28-day Keto Challenge*. This product offers a general plan for the Keto diet, explaining what it is and giving people a plan to use for eating during the first month of the diet.

This is a very useful product for people, but if you spend some time searching around the "*keto*" keyword on Clickbank, you're going to notice that there are many products that can serve as adjunct products to this one. So for example, as I showed you earlier, there was a Clickbank product that sold a ketogenic cookbook. There are also ketogenic supplements and different meal plans that supposedly tailor the Keto diet to your personal needs. With this in mind, one of the ways you can cross-sell is that after people buy the original product, you can move them to a separate email list that starts pitching a new related product to them, like a Keto cookbook or supplement.

There are endless opportunities to cross-sell related products. If you have looked into Keto dieting at all, you know that people that follow it also do intermittent fasting. So I looked on Clickbank, and lo and behold, I found a product for *Teaching Intermittent Fasting to Beginners*. So this is another product that you can slip into your email automation series.

If someone is interested in starting the Keto diet, they are going to be interested in *Intermittent Fasting* as well. That is guaranteed. So you can either put people on the new email list, or you can have one email list that pitches all items in a series. However, one thing I will say is that if you were pitching to people in a series, you might not get as many sales.

The reason that putting a bunch of products in a series is not as effective, is that first of all, you don't want to hard-sell people too much on your initial email list.

Second, the prospect becomes less warm as time goes on. So, most prospects on your list are going to buy right away. A month or six weeks or two months later, people that have not purchased something aren't necessarily the kind of prospects that you want to pitch to. So one way that I get around this problem, is that I move people from one list to another when they take some sort of action.

We could have three streams in our "keto" example. You might propose that you could move people who buy the first product on the Keto diet onto an email list that promotes *The Intermittent Fasting Method.* Then those who buy that book could be placed on an email list that pitches the cookbook. Or if you wanted to, you could move people to both lists at the same time. Certainly, someone who is interested in one of the products is going to be interested in all of them.

If you really wanted to get a solid business going on in this niche, something that I would do is I would sell all three products simultaneously. So you have one set going for *The 28-Day Keto Plan.* Then one for a *Keto Cookbook,* and the third you are marketing for *Intermittent Fasting.*

Then when someone buys *Intermittent Fasting,* you offer them *The 28-Day Keto Plan.* If someone buys *The 28-Day Keto Plan,* you offer them *Intermittent Fasting.* And you could do the same with customers that you are bringing in through the *Keto Cookbook* stream.

You can see that this offers you a great opportunity to expand your business. In short order, you can have multiple customers buying multiple products. So while you are starting out with a commission of $30 on each of your streams, you might end up with the average revenue per customer going well over $100. There are many other products that you can sell to these same customers – by also going outside the original niche.

What are people who are looking for a weight loss solution like keto also going to be interested in? Probably it'll be an exercise program. Or maybe they want to develop a rock hard stomach. Clickbank is full of many so-called "abs" products.

Many people interested in the Keto diet might also be diabetic. So you should also look at Clickbank to see if there are diabetes-related products you could sell these same customers.

This brings us to another important point: You should know who your customer is. You can do research on the niche to find out, and another way is to use Facebook audience insights if it can provide the data you need. Or you can take the hard and expensive but effective route – run your own Facebook ads and build up an audience that you can then profile for various characteristics.

When you know who your customers are – for example: How old is the average Keto dieter, and are they male or female? What Facebook pages are they most likely to follow? Are they diabetic? Then it is easier to advertise multiple products.

Keep in mind that when you stay close to the niche, you really don't need that level of detail. So in our original scenario, we looked at pitching three different Keto products to our lists. You can probably go ahead and just set that up. But if you are going to start expanding (such as into the diabetes niche) you will want to do more research.

Conclusion

Thank you very much for reading this book!

I am glad that you made it to the end and I hope that you have found the information in this book useful.

Online affiliate marketing provides a great opportunity to start your own home-based business. Moreover, it's a very flexible way to get into the business. An affiliate marketing business can be as small or as large as you want it to be. You can set up a system to make a modest extra few hundred dollars a month, or you can literally grow it into a large enterprise that pulls in a hefty seven figures. An affiliate marketing business can also be used as a springboard to creating and launching your own products. The sky is really the limit with affiliate marketing!

In this book, we have laid out all of the essential elements to setting up and running an affiliate marketing business. We have used Clickbank as an example, but you can use any affiliate network that you want to use. The essential elements include:

⇨ Choosing a niche. Select a niche that you are passionate about but that also has a good market size and needs.

- ⇨ Find a popular product to promote.
- ⇨ Pick a product when the vendor has tools to help you push their product.
- ⇨ Set up a blog, Facebook Page, and YouTube channel.
- ⇨ Learn how to cross-promote between all of your sites.
- ⇨ Setup a landing page and a sales funnel.
- ⇨ Create an email auto responder.
- ⇨ Create freebies for giveaways.
- ⇨ Use paid traffic
- ⇨ Start making money!

I hope that after reading this book you don't do what 99/100 people usually fail to do – TAKE ACTION. Those who actually take action on any kind of business are the ones who end up making money. You also will need to be persistent. You may get a sale quickly but most people have to work at it for awhile. So I hope that you will take action AND be persistent. Over time, you can help your business evolve into a passive income sales machine that can help you earn any amount of money that you can think of, provided that you take the right steps and put the work in.

Earning money online isn't necessarily easy or automatic, but I can certainly tell you this: It's the easiest way to make money from any kind of business. You don't have to keep inventory (if you don't want to), you can enter any kind of niche, and since its digital, you can scale it to become as large or small as you like without much effort and you can enter multiple niches simultaneously once you get yourself established.

I wish all readers all the best of luck. If you found this book informative, please drop by and give us a constructive review!

Justin A. Parker

Connect with us on our Facebook page www.facebook.com/bluesourceandfriends and stay tuned to our latest book promotions and free giveaways.